WRITING SURVIVAL SKILLS

FOR THE MIDDLE GRADES

by Imogene Forte
and
Joy MacKenzie

Incentive Publications, Inc.
Nashville, Tennessee

Graphics compiled by Angela C. Wilson
Cover by Geoffrey Brittingham
Edited by Sherri Y. Lewis

ISBN 0-86530-219-7

TABLE OF CONTENTS

Preface 7

Organizing For Study
  Parts I And II (Note-Taking And Organizing Material From Texts) 9
  Parts III - V (Note-Taking And Organizing Material
    From Lectures) 10

R-E-L-A-X (Getting Ready For Testing) 11

You Can Do It! (Making Study Sheets) 12

Superclues I (Taking Notes From Reading) 13

Superclues II (Taking Notes From Listening) 14

Sequencing Strips (Outlining) 15

The Well-Spelled Scholar (Studying Spelling) 16

Beware The Wolf! (Outlining) 17

Hot Topics! (Outlining) 19

It Takes A Writer
  ...To Tell The World (List-Making) 21
  ...To Create A Sign (Announcements/Posters) 22
  ...To Make The News (News Article/Classified Ad) 23
  ...And A Grand Time Was Had By All! (Feature Article/Report) 24

Instructions For Young Flyers (Writing Directions) 25

No Word Wasting Allowed! (Precise, Pictorial Messages) 27

Emergency! (Collecting And Writing Emergency Information) 29

Post A Thought (Creative Persuasive Posters) 31

Chain Gang (Pictorial Directions) 32

How-To-Hobby (Writing Sequential Instructions) 33

Getting There! (Writing Directions) 34

Meet Me At The Mall (Writing Directions) 35

Maps Make It Easier (Mapping Directions) 37

Proxy Parent (Completing Informational Forms) 38

Who's Who, Where, and When? (Informational Forms) 39

Application Jargon (Match Game) 40

Application Jargon (Application Form) 41

Job Wanted (Answering Want Ads) 42

Job Of The Moment (Employment Application-Specific) 43

Search For The "Right Stuff" (Employment Applications) 44

Write-On Résumé (Constructing A Résumé) 45

Career-Minded (Study Contract For Career Exploration) 47

This School Year Is In The Bag (Catalog Ordering) 48

How Well Do You Eat? (Record-Keeping) 50

Reading Log (Record-Keeping) 51

Weather-Wise (Charting) 52

Personal Property (Inventory) 54

You Light Up Their Lives (Special Occasions Planner) 55

Mini-messages (Memoranda) 56

Checkup (Writing Checks) 57

　　　　　 (Keeping A Register) 58

A Safe Deposit (Deposit Slips) 59

Anatomy Of A Biography (Collecting And Organizing Factual Data) 60

Biographical Data Work Sheet (Writing A Biography) 61

Editor's Guide (Editor's Checklist) 62

Publisher's Listing (Bibliography, Proofreading) 63

Study Guide (Bibliography Cards) 64

Proofreader's Marks 65

A Letter For A Friend (Form Of A Friendly Letter) 66

The Social Set (Social Notes) 67

Messages In Brief (Informal Notes) 68

A Glimpse Of Paradise (Postcards) 70

A Matter Of Business (Form Of A Business Letter) 71

Information Please (Business Letter) 73

Whoops! (Addressing A Business Envelope) 74

I'm Something Special (Autobiography) 75

Day By Day (Journal Writing) 76

Dear Diary (Journal Writing) 77

Make It Sparkle! (Sample Diary) 78

Today Is The Day (Diary) 79

Writing Skills Checklist 80

PREFACE

Teachers, administrators, and others responsible for planning and carrying out programs for middle grade students are becoming increasingly aware of the need to help students of this age level develop and use effective writing skills. Perhaps even more significant, they see, too, that the educational system is charged with the task of helping these same youngsters recognize the importance of writing proficiency to their normal everyday lives. Young adolescents of the 90s that react to the media-saturated world of hi-tech, high expectations, and high pressure often tend to look to computers, telephones, and audio/video devices as replacements for pencil, paper, books, and even conversation as a means of communication of ideas, knowledge, and information.

This book has been developed to provide middle grade students a series of practical experiences with everyday life skills that involve writing. Its purpose is to familiarize students with the kinds of writing tasks that will confront them on a daily basis and facilitate their survival as young adults in an increasingly aggressive and highly competitive world.

The format is skill-oriented and includes both teacher-directed and self-directed student activities. The design is "user-friendly" – it is written to the user and is presented in simple, sequential style requiring little outside preparation. The activities are based on topics of high interest and relevance to today's middle graders. They are designed to capture attention and challenge the imagination of students of this age, encourage more efficient and effective work habits, and result in improvement in the use of functional language skills and writing proficiency.

ORGANIZING FOR STUDY

PURPOSE:
Organizing information for study, testing.

PREPARATION:

1. Reproduce copies of R-E-L-A-X, SUPERCLUES I & II, and YOU CAN DO IT! – one of each per student.

2. Choose one section or chapter of a well-organized text in any subject area.

3. Prepare one or two brief (not more than 10 minute) lectures or demonstrations presenting material which supplements and/or highlights the text material.

PROCEDURE:

PART I

1. Distribute copies of R-E-L-A-X, YOU CAN DO IT!, and SUPERCLUES I to all students. Read together and discuss the recommended procedures. Let students add their ideas.

2. Direct students to skim the chosen text material. Together as a class, discuss the organization of the text and its "superclues." Ask individual students to point out what they consider to be important points.

3. Assign the text material to be read and organized for study, giving a deadline for study sheets to be completed.

PART II

4. On the due date, ask students to meet in groups of two or three, exchange study sheets, and evaluate and make suggestions regarding the improvement of each.

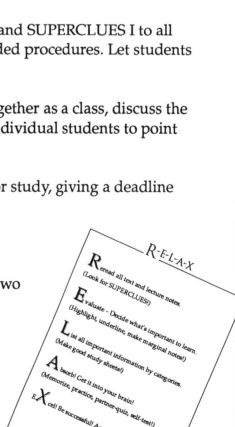

PART III

5. Distribute copies of SUPERCLUES II to all students. Read and discuss together as a class.

6. Ask students to get ready to take notes from a lecture/demonstration and present the teacher-prepared material.

7. Immediately, review together as a class the important information that was "noted" by different individuals and why. Then let students exchange papers with a partner and make any suggestions for improvement.

PART IV

8. After a suitable time for study (preferably on another day), TEST the text and lecture material.

9. "GRADE" the test together discussing where and how information for each item originated (text or lecture). Students will be amazed at how well they have "digested" the material and will be encouraged to use their study time in this organized fashion.

PART V

10. Repeat the entire process as often as needed (either with the entire class or with small groups of students who have more difficulty) until all students have gained fluency with the process.

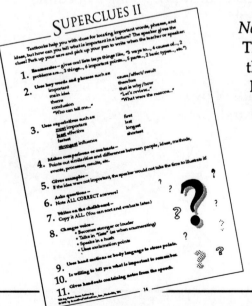

Note: The above activity is divided into five parts. The purpose of this is to provide opportunity for the teacher to tailor the activity to the particular learning situation (student ability levels, time allowances, etc.). Sections of the lesson should be conducted in sequence at the teacher's discretion.

R‑E‑L‑A‑X

Reread all text and lecture notes.
(Look for SUPERCLUES!)

Evaluate – Decide what's important to learn.
(Highlight, underline, make marginal notes!)

List all important information by categories.
(Make good study sheets!)

Absorb! Get it into your brain!
(Memorize, practice, partner-quiz, self-test!)

E**X**cel! Be successful! Ace the test!

YOU CAN DO IT!

I. CLASSIFY YOUR INFORMATION
Write all like things together on one sheet of paper.

Example: When classifying for a history test, you might have a page for each of the following:

names	superlatives (most, best, first, last, etc.)
places	definitions
vocabulary	dates (in order!)
main ideas	events (what, who, when, where?)
cause & effects	things that can be compared, contrasted

II. WRITE TO REMEMBER
(So you can take mental photographs!)

• Write on only ONE side of the page (easier to find).
• Use different colors of paper or pen (helps to visualize).
• Always put dates or events in chronological order.
• Group things that go together and leave space between groups.
• Put groups of single words in an easy-to-remember order.

Example: You might arrange lists of prepositions or chemical elements in alphabetical order.
To remember the names of the six New England states, you could make up a silly sentence or an acrostic:

Many **N**asty **V**ampires **M**ay **C**ause **R**iots.
E   H   T   A   T   I

A very old example is remembering how to spell the word "geography" by using this sentence:
<u>G</u>eorge <u>E</u>lliott's <u>o</u>ld <u>g</u>randfather <u>r</u>ode <u>a</u> <u>p</u>ig <u>h</u>ome <u>y</u>esterday!
This method of remembering things is called "mnemonics." (That's pronounced "nee-mon-icks.")

As you review your study sheets, **highlight, underline, star, color-code**, etc., ANYTHING to help picture it in your mind!

III. TEST YOURSELF – *over and over...*
Use your study sheets to:
LOOK and SAY – **Look** at the term, **say** the definition.
COVER and PEEK – **Cover** part of the list and say it; **peek** to check!
PARTNER QUIZ – Trade study sheets and "test" with a classmate.
MAKE MENTAL SNAPSHOTS – Close your eyes. See if you can visualize the group of words on the page and say them aloud to yourself. (It helps to hear them, too!)

SUPERCLUES I

Taking Notes From A Text

When the teacher assigns a summary or report to be written on part of a textbook or when you have one or more chapters of a text to study for a test, HOW does a student figure out what's important to include in study notes? Sometimes it's a great mystery, but cheer up! There are some **superclues** hidden in those books! Try this:

Get two or three of your textbooks. (Social studies, science, and English grammar texts are usually the best examples.)

LOOK FOR CLUES – words or phrases that are written or spaced  differently on a page than the rest of the writing on the page.

- big print
- all capital letters
- bold, heavy print
- colored print
- underlined print
- phrases in which each word is capitalized (Boston Tea Party)

- words in italics
- words/phrases marked with numbers/letters
- word lists
- first word or phrase after a white space
- captions under pictures or diagrams

These are usually main ideas or very important things to remember. Underline or highlight them (if possible) in your text. Copy them into your notebook!

LOOK FOR A REVIEW SECTION – usually at the end of each chapter.

- vocabulary words
- summaries
- problems to solve

- study questions
- self-tests
- assignments

Read carefully and go over the questions and activities in this section to check your knowledge. If the review shows you have missed any important ideas in the text, add them to your study notes NOW. If the authors of the book thought this stuff was important, the teacher probably thinks so, too!

Review

SUPERCLUES II

Taking Notes From A Lecture

Textbooks help you with clues for locating important words, phrases, and ideas, but how can you tell what is important in a lecture? The speaker gives the clues! Perk up your ears and pick up your pen to write when the teacher or speaker:

1. **Enumerates** – gives oral lists (says things like, "3 ways to..., 4 causes of..., 2 problems are..., 3 things..., 6 important points..., 5 parts..., 2 basic types..., etc.")

2. **Uses key words and phrases** such as:

important	cause/effect/result
main idea	therefore
theme	that is why/how
conclusion	"Let's review..."
"Who can tell me..."	"What were the reasons..."

3. **Uses superlatives** such as:

<u>most</u> important	first
<u>least</u> effective	last
fastest	longest
<u>strongest</u> influence	shortest

4. **Makes comparisons or contrasts** –
Points out similarities and differences between people, ideas, methods, events, processes, results, etc.

5. **Gives examples** –
If the idea were not important, the speaker would not take the time to illustrate it!

6. **Asks questions** –
Note ALL CORRECT answers!

7. **Writes on the chalkboard** –
Copy it ALL. (You can sort and evaluate later.)

8. **Changes voice** –
- Becomes stronger or louder
- Talks in "lists" (as when enumerating)
- Speaks in a hush
- Uses exclamation points

9. **Uses hand motions or body language to stress points.**

10. **Is willing to tell you what is important to remember.**

11. **Gives handouts containing notes from the speech.**

Taking Notes From Listening
© 1991 by Incentive Publications, Inc., Nashville, TN.

SEQUENCING STRIPS

The sentences below represent three main ideas related to one topic. For each main idea, there are three supporting details. Cut the page on the dotted lines and separate the sentence strips. Then use paste to attach each strip on a clean, separate sheet of paper in the appropriate order.

I enjoy the feeling of speed when water skiing.

I have a huge library of rock and roll tapes and CDs.

Three special interests occupy most of my time outside of school.

My own horses are a chestnut Arabian and a thoroughbred.

I have a strong interest in music.

Snorkeling allows me to see the exciting underwater world.

I am a real horse lover.

My friends and I are trying to start a band.

Things I Like A Lot.

I collect books about horse breeding.

Saturdays are reserved for sailing!

My bedroom wall is covered with posters of rock groups.

Training for the Olympic horse trials is a future dream of mine.

I love participating in water sports!

THE WELL-SPELLED SCHOLAR

How are you as a speller? Really good, just OK, a real loser, or absolutely fantastic? To find out, test yourself on the spelling list below. Read each word carefully to be sure you can pronounce it correctly and know its meaning. Look up any unfamiliar ones in the dictionary.

arctic	governor	library	picture	lightning
drowned	athlete	burglar	surprise	February
all right	biscuit	nickel	describe	history
every	attacked	popular	electric	extraordinary
separate	receive	expense	restaurant	generally
hoping	bargain	definitely	yesterday	colonel
shining	family	regular	usually	Wednesday
film	column	quiet	burst	chief

Now record the spelling list on a tape recorder, dictating each word slowly and clearly. When the entire list has been recorded, play it back to yourself as a spelling test. Write the words on a piece of paper. Then, check your test paper by comparing it with this list. Place an "X" by each word that you missed, and study those words carefully. Take the test again, and mark any missed words. Keep working until you are able to spell the entire word list. Use this study guide to help you.

HOW TO STUDY A SPELLING WORD

1. Look carefully at the whole word.
2. Be sure you understand its meaning.
3. Say it aloud, pronouncing each syllable distinctly.
4. Look at each syllable again to find expected trouble spots.
5. Shut your eyes and try to visualize the word.
6. Look at the word and write it saying each letter as you write.
7. Write the word again without looking at your list.
8. Check to see that you've spelled it correctly.
9. Repeat all the steps until you've mastered each word.

BEWARE THE WOLF!

Outlining a text requires careful reading and thinking. Always read the entire text first, looking only for **topic sentences** or **main ideas**. (Ask yourself: What is the **big message** in this paragraph?) Underline the sentence or phrase that best states the main idea. Then go back and look for sentences that support the main ideas. (There may be one or many.) Try your skill with this piece about *Red Riding Hood*.

1. Write the **big message** beside Roman numeral **I** on the next page.

2. Write the two **main ideas** beside capital letters **A** and **B**.

3. Then reread to get **supporting details** for A and B and write these on the numbered lines **1** and **2** under each letter.

4. When you have finished, give the outline a clever **title**.

Note: Read carefully. Details are not always in the exact order of the outline. Don't be fooled by the wolf!

BEWARE THE WOLF!

Name _____

     Red Riding Hood's assailant was a deceitful, malicious character! Tall, dark, and handsome, he misrepresented himself by posing as a kindly gentleman. When he approached Miss Hood in the woods, he offered to help her carry her basket and politely inquired about her destination. Underneath, he was ruthless and violent. He forced his way into Hood's grandmother's house, threw the elderly lady into a closet, stole her clothes and her identity, and waited for Hood's arrival. When the girl arrived, he deceived her by mimicking her grandmother's voice and lured her to his side. Then he leaped on her with the intention of devouring her. Had a passing hunter not heard her screams, Miss Hood would have surely been dinner for the vicious wolf.

I. _____

   A. _____

      1. _____

      2. _____

   B. _____

      1. _____

      2. _____

   C. _____

      1. _____

      2. _____

HOT TOPICS

PURPOSE:
Outlining researched material

PREPARATION:

1. Make one copy of the HOT TOPICS work sheet for each student.

2. Make arrangements for library research time, or provide classroom time, space, and materials including information related to the "hot" topics.

PROCEDURE:

1. Choose one subject from the HOT TOPICS list:

Sunburns	Arson	Bakeries	Volcanoes	Fireworks
Fire-eaters	Fever	Lightning	Fire fighting	Politics

2. Engage students in the task of creating a probable topic sentence related to the chosen subject. Write it on the chalkboard as Roman numeral I of an outline.

3. Ask students to join you in creating a possible outline by identifying two or three main ideas or areas of investigation related to the topic. List these in topical outline form (A,B,C) on the board.

4. If possible, think of several supporting details that might be added as 1, 2, etc., under each main idea. Otherwise, leave these numbers blank and discuss what **kinds** of ideas might belong there.

5. Distribute the HOT TOPICS work sheet to students. Ask them to choose the subject of most interest to them and develop either a topic or sentence outline (or both).

6. Arrange for partner or small group conference time when students may share their outlines for peer evaluation.

7. Arrange a subsequent time for teacher/student evaluation and reteaching time for those students who need additional help.

HOT TOPICS!

Name _____

Sunburns	Arson	Bakeries	Volcanoes	Fireworks
Fire-eaters	Fever	Lightning	Fire fighting	Politics

1. Choose one of the "hot topics" above. Write a sentence that states the big idea or message you will research. Write it next to Roman numeral I.

2. Choose three main ideas related to the big topic. Write a topic sentence for each, and enter it on the outline under A, B, or C.

3. Find at least two details that support each idea. List them as 1, 2, etc., on the outline.

I. _____

   A. _____

      1. _____

      2. _____

   B. _____

      1. _____

      2. _____

   C. _____

      1. _____

      2. _____

IT TAKES A WRITER...
TO TELL THE WORLD

Name _____

The date for the school bake sale and pet show has finally been set. You have been appointed publicity chairman.

Here are the notes from the committee planning session. Read the notes carefully. Then make a list of all the ways you can think of to get publicity.

Bake Sale and Pet Show Notes

• Saturday, March 29, from 9 a.m. until 4 p.m. on the school play-ground – in the auditorium if it rains.

• Admission free – everyone invited.

• Something for all ages.

• Pies, cakes, cookies, candy for sale.

• Pet show on tennis court at 1 p.m.

• Any student can enter pet in show.

• Grand prize is $25 gift certificate from Henson's Pet Mall.

• Second prize is 2 tickets to Sea Scape Marineland.

• Soft drinks, hot dogs, balloons, and stuffed toys will be for sale in booths.

Ways to get Publicity

IT TAKES A WRITER...
TO CREATE A SIGN

Name _____

      Your very first job is to create a sign to be placed downtown on Main Street to advertise the big occasion.

      Don't forget to check the committee notes for the correct time, place, and special events of the bake sale and pet show. Make the sign so attractive that everybody in town will want to come.

IT TAKES A WRITER...
TO MAKE THE NEWS

Name _____

      Use the committee notes from TO TELL THE WORLD to write an article to appear in the local newspaper. Then create a five-sentence classified ad to appear in the same edition.

      Remember to include all information related to the event in both the article and the ad.

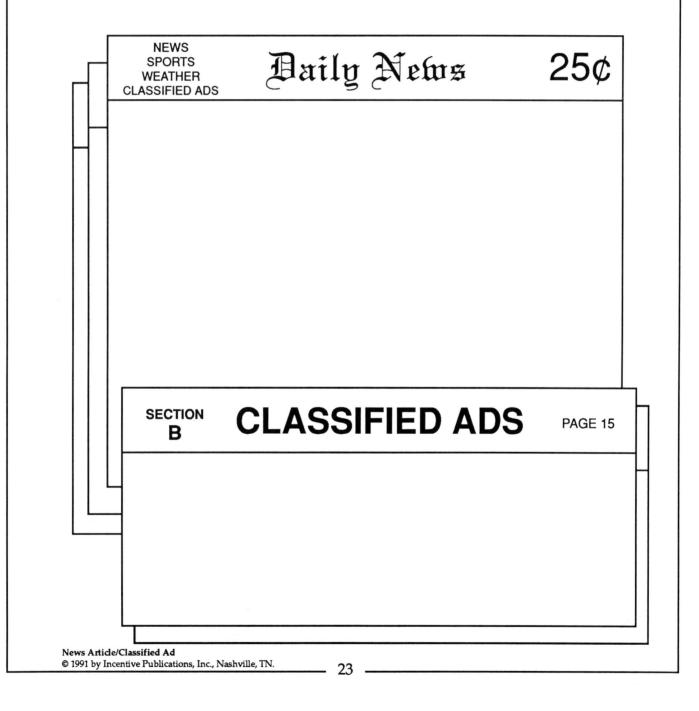

IT TAKES A WRITER...

AND A GRAND TIME WAS HAD BY ALL!

Name _____

    Well, you did such a marvelous job as publicity chairman of the bake sale/pet show that you have been asked to write the first report to go on file in the official school record book.

    In addition to the time, place, and other information included in the committee notes, here is the information you will need to include in the report.

- 725 people attended
- $940 was collected
- 46 pets were entered in the pet show.
- First prize went to Billy Slayton's poodle.
- Second prize went to Kristen Dalton's calico cat.
- Next year, the hot dog booth should be open earlier as many people said they would like to eat lunch before the pet show.

INSTRUCTIONS FOR YOUNG FLYERS

A group of third graders wants to learn to make paper airplanes. You have offered to write the directions for them. Using the illustrated diagrams as a guide, write directions in each of the corresponding boxes on the work sheet. Write your directions clearly and completely so that they can easily be followed without the diagram.

Writing Directions
© 1991 by Incentive Publications, Inc., Nashville, TN.

YOUNG FLYERS

Name _____

1.

2.

3.

4.

5.

6.

7.

8.

9.

NO WORD WASTING ALLOWED!

Name _____

   Sometimes it is important to be able to write messages in the fewest words possible.

   Read each of the messages below. Then draw a sign and use no more than three words in each to convey the meaning of each written message.

Example: You can reach the airport by going one mile straight down this road.

1 Mile

This parking space is to be used by handicapped persons only.

This wall has just been painted.

All cars must come to a complete stop at this intersection.

The exit for Interstate 65 is only one mile from here.

In case of fire, people should leave through this rear door.

Hamburgers are for sale here. They cost $1.

Drivers are requested to drive slowly and carefully through these three blocks because of the school.

WORD WASTING

Name _____

    These are signs with few or no words. Write the intended message in a complete sentence beside each sign.

    Isn't it amazing how one small picture or just a few words can communicate a very important message?

_____

_____

_____

_____

_____

_____

_____

_____

_____

_____

DETOUR

X-ING

EMERGENCY!

PURPOSE:
Creating an emergency information center.

PREPARATION:

Reproduce one copy of the EMERGENCY! work sheet for each student.

PROCEDURE:

1. Discuss with students the need for clear, concise, direct information in emergency situations.

2. Point out that emergencies often require quick thinking and immediate action. A prearranged center where family members can quickly locate easy-to-read emergency phone numbers and clear information can save valuable time and perhaps a life!

3. Distribute copies of the EMERGENCY! work sheets and ask students to think of any additional information that might be needed for their particular home situation. For instance, under the caption "Remember!" they may need to note special medical conditions or allergies such as: Dad is diabetic; Joni has asthma; Bud is allergic to penicillin, etc.

4. Direct students to use any or all of the pictures and words on the work sheet, poster board, and art supplies to cut, paste, and create an EMERGENCY! miniposter for their family. They will need a telephone directory to add correct numbers. Encourage neatness and large, readable lettering. They should consult their families about choosing an appropriate place to display their poster at home.

EMERGENCY!

Emergency Numbers

Police _____

Fire _____

Ambulance _____

Doctor _____

Hospital _____

Poison Center _____

Relative _____

Neighbor _____

What to say:
(Speak slowly and distinctly.)
This is an emergency!
My name is _____ .

My address is _____ .

The problem is _____ .

REMEMBER! (Add any additional information your family may need.)

POST A THOUGHT

Name _____

Posters are often designed to influence people's beliefs, values, or behavior.

Design a poster to influence other people to do one of the following things:

1. Use the public library.
2. Learn to swim.
3. Hug their kids.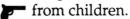
4. Save money.
5. Curb their dog.
 6. Vote in the next city election.

7. Conserve natural resources.
8. Wear seatbelts.
9. Quit smoking.
10. Say no to drugs.
11. Recycle trash.
12. Keep firearms away from children.

Make up a catchy, one-line caption, short poem, or jingle. Use it with a clever, attractive illustration to carry your message.

CHAIN GANG

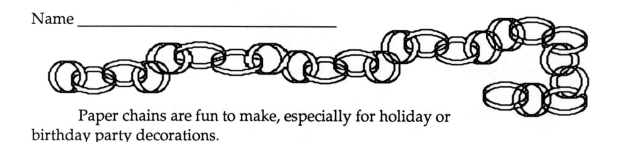

Name _____

Paper chains are fun to make, especially for holiday or birthday party decorations.

Select a kind of chain you'd like to make. Gather the necessary art supplies, and make a chain that is your very own in color, shape, size, kind of paper, length, etc.

When your chain is complete, look at it carefully and draw pictures to show someone who neither reads nor speaks English how to make the chain. Remember, you will have to picture the supplies and every step in your construction.

Name _____

Mary Mixup is in a mess again. Saturday is the day of the hobby fair, and Mary is working frantically to get her entry ready. Since she is a creative person who likes to work with her hands, the bird feeder she plans to enter has been done for days. It looks great. Mary's problem is organization. She has problems writing the step-by-step direction card that is required. Your job is to put the jumbled-up steps in order and complete the card.

Mary's notes:

You make a string loop to hang the bird feeder from a tree branch after you have used scissors to cut out a square opening in two sides of the milk carton. Punch holes in the sides of the carton, and run a small tree branch through the opening for the bird to perch on. The last thing you do is put in some bird seed. I painted it to make it look pretty. I also added some tiny paper bugs and flowers as decorations.

HOW TO MAKE A
BIRD FEEDER:

Materials:

Directions:

Getting There!

Name _____

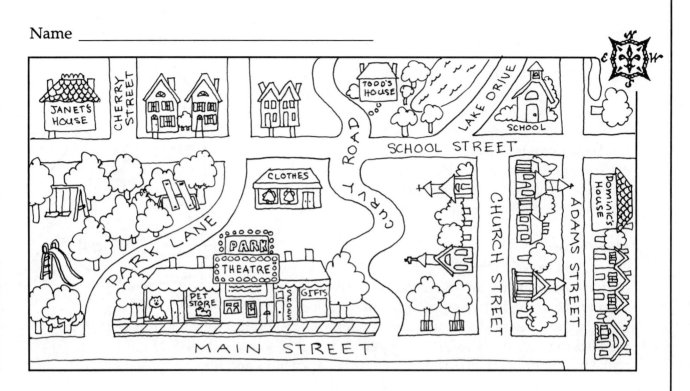

The new science-fiction movie *The Plant Eater* is showing at the Park Theater in the Main Street Shopping Center. Dominic, Todd, and Janet plan to meet at the theater Saturday afternoon to see it, but none of them is sure just where the building is.

Read the map shown here. Then help the three friends get to the movie by making each of them a set of written directions from home to the theater.

Janet	Todd	Dominic

MEET ME AT THE MALL

Name _____

Use the mall directory work sheet to find answers to the questions following each situation.

Situation 1 – Jody wanted Sally to meet him at the Sunrise Bakery.

Jody's Directions – Enter from the red parking area. Walk past the Kandy Kitchen and Today Theater. Turn right at Write's Stationery Shop and then left at Classy Cleaners. The bakery is at the end of the walkway.

Are these directions correct? _____ If not, circle the incorrect part of the directions, and write the correction here.

_____

_____

Situation 2 – Tony wanted to buy a bicycle rack at Toy Town. He asked the guard in the blue parking area for directions.

Guard's Directions – Walk past the Flower Cart, and turn left at Dora's Dress Shop. Enter Toy Town on the right.

Are these directions correct? _____ What directions would the guard have given Tony if they had been in the red parking area?

_____

_____

Situation 3 – Jennifer invited Tom to go shopping and see a movie. She told him to meet her at the Today Theater at noon.

Jennifer's Directions – Park in the green parking area. Walk past Toy Town, Dora's Dress Shop, and the Flower Cart. Enter the theater through the door by the fountain.

Are Jennifer's directions correct? _____ Write another set of directions that will tell Tom a different route to Today Theater.

_____

_____

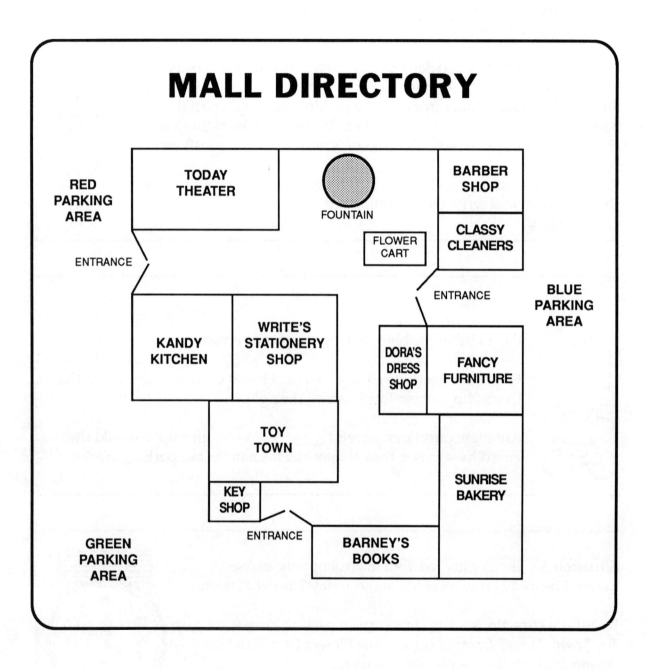

MALL DIRECTORY

RED PARKING AREA

TODAY THEATER

FOUNTAIN

BARBER SHOP

FLOWER CART

CLASSY CLEANERS

ENTRANCE

ENTRANCE

BLUE PARKING AREA

KANDY KITCHEN

WRITE'S STATIONERY SHOP

DORA'S DRESS SHOP

FANCY FURNITURE

TOY TOWN

KEY SHOP

SUNRISE BAKERY

GREEN PARKING AREA

ENTRANCE

BARNEY'S BOOKS

Writing Directions
© 1991 by Incentive Publications, Inc., Nashville, TN.

MAPS MAKE IT EASIER

Name _____

     Draw a map for each of the shopping situations in the MEET ME AT THE MALL activity. Use only pictures, words, and directional lines that are absolutely necessary for each situation.

Situation #1

Situation #2

Situation #3

PROXY PARENT

A proxy is a substitute for someone else. In this activity, you are asked to be a proxy for your parent or guardian. Schools require that parents and guardians complete an official information form such as the one below for each student. Pretend that you are your mother, father, or guardian and complete the form as he/she would for you.

PUPIL INFORMATION FORM*

Pupil's Name _____
(Last)   (First)   (Middle)

Date of Birth: Month _____ Day _____ Year _____ Sex: M ❑ F ❑

Place of Birth _____

Name of Parent or Guardian _____ Phone _____

Address _____
(Street / Apt. Number)   (Street Name)

_____
(City)   (State)   (Zip)

With whom is pupil now living? _____ Relationship _____

Father (or Guardian)	Mother (or Guardian)
Full Name _____	Full Name _____
Place of Employment _____	Place of Employment_____
Occupation_____	Occupation _____
Father's Work Phone _____	Mother's Work Phone _____
Family Physician _____	Phone_____
Pupil's Years in School _____	General Health Conditions _____

_____

Does pupil have any seeing, hearing, or speech problems? _____

If so, explain _____

*If any question does not apply to your family, write NA in the space provided.

WHO'S WHO, WHERE, AND WHEN?

In order to provide a pleasant, well-organized place where students and faculty can live and work together, schools must have all kinds of written information on file. They are responsible for every moment of each student's school day. That's why there are so many pieces of paper to fill out. See how quickly and accurately you can complete this one for the principal's file.

					Grade
					Birthday
					Sex
Last Name	First	Middle	Advisor	Locker #	Race

_____
Name of Parent (Guardian)

Address _____

_____

Phone _____

Emergency # _____

Parent/Guardian Occupation: _____

_____

Family Doctor _____

Phone _____

DAILY SCHEDULE

Subject	Period	Teacher
	1	
	2	
	3	
	4	
	5	
	6	
	7	
	8	
	9	

(Use this space to add something you'd like your principal to know about you.)

Now have a little fun! Pretend you are the official designer of forms for your school. Use the space below to create a form for one or more of the following, or make up one of your own.

Request for a Day Off
   (1 per student per year)
Request for a Math Holiday
   (1 per student per quarter)
Hall Pass
Library Card
Lunch Ticket

Informational Forms
© 1991 by Incentive Publications, Inc., Nashville, TN.

Application Jargon

Name _____

Application forms have a jargon all their own. ("Jargon" is a special group of words that "go with" only a certain topic, like applications!) Application jargon contains words that are often used to ask for information. Before you try to complete any application form, you need to become familiar with these terms. See how many you already know by playing the match game below. (Turn your paper upside down for help in completing those you do not know.)

Match Game

___ 1. Surname
___ 2. Given name
___ 3. Maiden name
___ 4. Initial
___ 5. Residence
___ 6. Zip code
___ 7. Marital status
___ 8. Birthdate
___ 9. Birthplace
___ 10. Sex
___ 11. Race
___ 12. Spouse
___ 13. Nationality
___ 14. Occupation
___ 15. Education
___ 16. Experience
___ 17. Salary
___ 18. Reference
___ 19. Physician
___ 20. Emergency number
___ 21. Social security number

A. The country of which a person is a citizen.
B. First letter of a word in a name.
C. Day, month, and year a person was born.
D. What a person does for a job.
E. A person who knows you well.
F. A person's last name.
G. Address or place where a person lives.
H. List of jobs a person has had.
I. A person's first name.
J. A 5-digit number that identifies postal areas in the United States.
K. A woman's last name before she marries.
L. The amount of money paid for a job.
M. Telephone number to call in case of accident or illness.
N. Single, married, or divorced.
O. Male or female.
P. Place where a person was born.
Q. Ethnic group as defined by physical characteristics (black, white, Asian, etc.).
R. Number of school years completed.
S. A person's husband or wife.
T. Identification number assigned by the government.
U. A person's doctor.

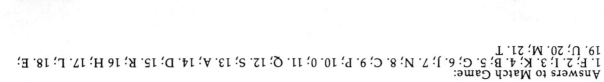

Answers to Match Game:
1. F; 2. I; 3. K; 4. B; 5. G; 6. J; 7. N; 8. C; 9. P; 10. O; 11. Q; 12. S; 13. A; 14. D; 15. R; 16 H; 17. L; 18. E; 19. U; 20. M; 21. T.

APPLICATION JARGON

Use what you have learned to complete the application form.

PLEASE PRINT

Name _____ Birthdate _____
        Surname   Given Name   Initial

Residence _____ Phone (____) _____

_____ Soc. Security # _____

Birthplace _____ Sex ____ Race_____

Nationality _____ Present Occupation _____

Name of Spouse _____ Spouse's Occupation _____

Name and Address of Nearest Relative not Living with You_____

_____

Emergency Number _____ Physician's Name _____

Education: (Circle highest completed.)   Gr. 6   Gr. 8   H.S.   College

Previous Job Experience:_____

_____

Expected Salary _____

REFERENCES

1. _____
        Name   Address   Phone

2. _____
        Name   Address   Phone

_____
                                    Your Signature

JOB WANTED

Name _____

Select the summer job from the want ads below that would be interesting to you.

Write a letter applying for the job. Remember, applications should be brief and to the point. Give your qualifications in five sentences or less.

Kids needed to pull weeds & cut grass 9 to 3, 5 days/week, $4 per hour. Apply to B. Bascalupo. Public Parks, Dept. 6F, Freeport, FL 33289

Boy to deliver packages. Bicycle a must - 9 to 5, Mon. through Sat. Good pay! Apply by letter to J. Swingbottom, Handy's Dept. Store, Public Square, Cold Springs, VT 01089

Dependable & considerate boy or girl to run errands & be summer companion for elderly man 10 to 2, 6 days a week. Lovely home: lunch furnished. $50 per week. Write Mr. T.S. Jamison, 604 Commerce St., Waco, TX 77067

Ambitious girl needed to assist beautician at Barbara's Beauty Box, 7011 Lucky Blvd., Main Chance, MD 06435

Dishwashers needed! Petro's Diner, 604 N. Main St., Sunnyvale, MI 48009. Evelyn Scruggs, mgr. Hours flexible, 5 hours per day, $12.50. No experience required.

Young people needed to work with 4-yr.-old kids at Betty Booper Day-Care Ctr. 4 hours/day, either AM or PM. Salary set by qualifications. Ms. Jo James, Dir., 604 Ivey St., St. Thomas, RI 00342

JOB OF THE MOMENT

Iva Moment lives with her parents Mr. and Mrs. Justa Moment at ninety-nine hundred River Road in St. Thomas, Rhode Island. Her zip code is 00342, and her phone number is 934-4670. She is 12-years-old, a brunette with blue eyes, weighs 86 pounds, and is four feet, ten inches tall. She has just finished the sixth grade at St. Andrew's School and is a straight A student, except for physical education. Since she likes to read a lot and is not especially interested in sports or games, she does not do well in this area.

Last summer, she worked as a clean-up girl two days a week at Barbara's Beauty Box. During the school year, she baby-sat for the Jones' children next door for $2 an hour. This summer, she has secured her parents' permission to apply for a few jobs in her own neighborhood. She is especially interested in the day-care position because she likes kids and thinks she would be a good teacher's helper.

Fill out this application for her.

Newspaper clipping: Hours flexible, 5 hours per day. $16.00. No experience required. Young people needed to work with 4-yr.-old kids at Betty Boope Day Care Ctr. 4 hours/day, either A.M. or P.M. Salary set by qualifications. Ms. Jo James, Dir., 604 Ivey St., St. Thomas, RI 00342

Betty Boope Day-Care Center Application for Employment

Name _____ Phone (_____) _____

Address _____

Age _____ Weight _____ Height _____

Job applied for _____

Education _____

Special talents that qualify you for this position _____

_____

_____

Past experience _____

_____

Salary expected _____

References: Person   Address

_____

_____

Give a three sentence statement telling why you want this job.

_____

_____

_____

SEARCH FOR THE "RIGHT STUFF"

PURPOSE:
Completing employment applications.

PREPARATION:

1. Collect current employment application forms from as many sources as possible. Try to include those from firms in your area that employ young people – fast food places, a car wash, a department store, library, bookstore, supermarkets, etc.

2. Get permission from the firms to make enough copies to supply each student with one or two applications.

3. Provide poster board, construction paper, markers, scissors, and paste for creating signs.

4. Prepare a display area where students can share their finished products.

PROCEDURE:

1. Instruct students to read carefully the applications they have chosen, completing the forms mentally – no writing required. Ask them to highlight or list on a separate sheet of paper any word or phrase on the application forms they do not fully understand.

2. As a class, make a composite list of these difficulties on the chalkboard and discuss or research to find solutions to questions.

3. When it is apparent that students are familiar with the application form jargon and have an understanding of the kinds of information needed by employers to locate appropriate workers for their firms, divide the class into groups of three or four.

4. Direct each group to work together to form a "company" or "firm" which will hire a group of employees. Their task as a group is to choose a business or service, create a company name and logo, and make a sign that might appear on the building where their business might be housed.

5. The group must then work together to develop an application form for employment in their company requesting all the necessary information they feel would be needed to locate good, reliable employees for their business. The application must be presented in neat, readable, "professional" form.

6. When signs and application forms are complete, they may be displayed together in the prepared area where students should be given time to browse and enjoy one another's contributions.

7. A follow-up evaluation/discussion of students' products should follow.

WRITE-ON RÉSUMÉ

A résumé contains much of the same information as an application, but it is different because there is no form to fill out. On a résumé, you get to decide how to present information about yourself, but you must be careful to include everything the reader needs to know plus everything you would like him/her to know about you. If you want to impress your reader, the presentation must be neat and orderly.

A résumé is usually organized in broad topics. The information can be in list or paragraph form or a combination of the two. Notice that the headings are written in large or darker print than the specific information.

Introduction of Applicant
Name, Address, Phone, Sex, Race, Nationality
Birthdate, Age, Marital Status, Social Security Number

Personal History
Family
Special Talents, Abilities

Educational Background
Schooling
Other preparation or qualifications for this job.

Work Experience
Other jobs or positions you have had.

Job Objectives
Why you want this job.
Why you think you would be a good person to fill this job.

References
Names, addresses, and occupations of several people who know you well and can tell about your personal character and your job qualifications.

Use the work sheet WRITE-ON RÉSUMÉ to create your own résumé. You may make it a true statement of yourself today, or pretend that you are 35-years-old, and make up information about your "future" self.

———————————————— BONUS! ————————————————
For fun, use a blank copy of the WRITE-ON RÉSUMÉ page to create a résumé for one of these fictitious people:

Elmer Fudd, Fred Flintstone, Superman, Big Bad Wolf, Goliath, Batman, The Grinch, Lucy, Charlie Brown, Bugs Bunny, Cinderella, Robin Hood, etc.

Constructing A Résumé
© 1991 by Incentive Publications, Inc., Nashville, TN.

WRITE-ON RÉSUMÉ

Introduction

_____

Personal History

_____

Educational Background

_____

Work Experience

_____

Job Objectives

_____

References

CAREER-MINDED

My name _____

Career to be explored _____

I chose this career because _____

_____

Books and periodicals I will read _____

_____

Other sources of information I will use _____

Field trips, resource people, and other activities _____

_____

My project will be completed by _____

I will present my project to the class on _____

I will present my project to the class by
- ❏ drama
- ❏ lecture
- ❏ notebook
- ❏ video
- ❏ handouts
- ❏ other _____

I will have a conference with the teacher on _____

I would like my project evaluated in the following way _____

_____
Signature

_____
Teacher's Signature

_____
Date

THIS SCHOOL YEAR IS IN THE BAG

Name _____

This is an order blank from a catalog your teacher might use to order materials for your classroom. Look around your room, and take inventory of the materials and supplies on hand. Think of the kinds of things you like to do and the materials needed to do them. From the listings in the bags on the following page, make out an order that you would like your teacher to send. Use your teacher's name and school address on the order form.

The BCD Company
9432 General Philpot Dr.
Morningside, MT 56803
Phone: (406) 924-4612

Order Blank
BCD-98

Please Print or Type

Ship To: Name _____
School _____
Address _____
City/State/Zip _____
Phone # ( ) _____

Quantity (State by unit of sale: Each; Pkg.; etc., as in catalog.)	Product	Price Per Catalog Unit	Extension (Total)

Shipping charges vary greatly depending on type and weight of merchandise. Please include 10% of the merchandise value for shipping.

Merchandise Total	
Shipping Charges	
Applicable Sales Tax	
Total	

Please pay **FULL** amount due.

THIS SCHOOL YEAR IS IN THE BAG

MATH
Math-O-Matic Games ... $6.00
Math Workbook $3.00
Giant Math Quiz book .. $9.00
Math Skills Sheets $6.00
Hard Math $8.00
Easy Math $8.00

ART SUPPLIES
Magic Crayons (box of 24) $3.50
Super Clay (3 lb. box) $5.00
Felt-Tip Pens (1 dz.) $6.50
Poster Paint (carton) $5.00
Tagboard (per sheet) $1.00
Drawing Paper (1 pkg.) $2.50
Poster Paper (1 pkg.) $3.00
Tissue Paper (1 pkg.) $3.50
Glue (1 dz.) $12.00
Mural Paper (1 roll) $24.00

READING, SPELLING
Reading Workbook $3.50
Reading Game Book $7.50
Crossword Puzzle Book $5.50
Spelling Work Sheets (1 pkg.) $4.00
Poetry Pickings Book $6.50
Guide to the Library $3.90
Scrabble® Game $14.95
Brand
Pictionary® Game $16.00

SCIENCE
Test Tubes (1 pkg.) $5.00
Microscope $100.00
Wonders of Science Book $6.50
Science Game book $5.00
Rock & Crystal Set $40.00
Ant Farm $16.95
Bird Feeder $14.50
Weather Instruments (set) $60.00

GOODIES
Chalk (pastel – 1 pkg.) $1.90
Multicolored Yarn $2.00
(1 pkg.)
Wall Calendar $5.00
Game Assortment $10.00
(4 per pkg.)

WRITING
Lined Paper (1 pkg.) $6.00
Handwriting Guide $7.00
Storystarter Book $5.50
Dictionary $9.00
Thesaurus $8.00
Calligraphy Pens (set of 2) ... $12.00

PHYS ED AND MUSIC
Baseball, Glove, Hat $24.00
Frisbee® $3.00
Game Book $6.00
Volleyball and Net $12.00
Melody Record $6.50
Rhythm Band Instruments $27.00
Hacky-Sak® $12.00
Music Video (set of 4) $96.00
Tether Ball Set.................. $36.00

HOW WELL DO YOU EAT?

Name _____

Most people today are becoming more concerned about eating the right foods to build strong, healthy bodies. One of the first steps toward establishing good eating habits is to find out what really is being eaten.

Use this form to keep a record of all the food you eat this week. Don't forget to include snacks.

	BREAKFAST	LUNCH	DINNER
SUNDAY			
MONDAY			
TUESDAY			
WEDNESDAY			
THURSDAY			
FRIDAY			
SATURDAY			

At the end of the week, circle all the "healthy" meals that you ate, and draw a line through the "junk food" meals.

Compare the two. How healthy are your eating habits?

──────────────────── BONUS: ────────────────────

Use a copy of the above chart to keep track of all the fat grams or calories you consume in one week. Check boxes and labels on food items to get the information you need. You can also find a helpful book or magazine article in the library.

READING LOG

Name _____

Week of _____ Goal (Number of books) _____

Keep a record of books you read to help you evaluate your reading progress while
improving the use of record-keeping skills.

DATE	WHAT I'M READING	PAGES	WHAT IT'S ABOUT	1-3 WORD EVALUATION

NEW AND
DIFFICULT WORDS
I'VE DISCOVERED!

Record-Keeping © 1991 by Incentive Publications, Inc., Nashville, TN.

WEATHER-WISE

PURPOSE:

Practicing pictorial writing/graphs.

PREPARATION:

1. Prepare a large chart or bulletin board using the projected temperature readings for your vicinity for five school days. Attach yarn and pins as shown.

2. Provide a weather thermometer and place it in the closest possible outdoor area convenient to the classroom.

3. Reproduce the WEATHER-WISE work sheet for the participants.

PROCEDURE:

1. Lead a class discussion related to the temperature.

2. At the same time each day, read the thermometer, and attach the yarn to show the correct temperature.

3. Culminate the study on Friday by distributing copies of the WEATHER-WISE work sheet. Direct students to show the temperature for the five days by using the marked chart to fill in the graph and to complete the rest of the work sheet.

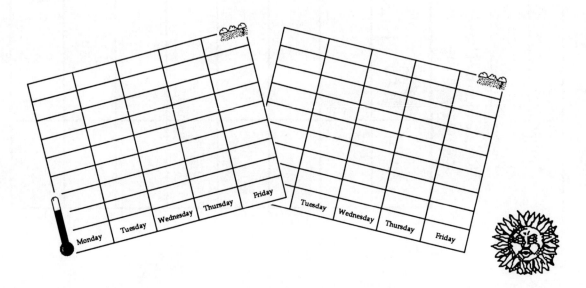

WEATHER-WISE WORK SHEET

Name _____

Fill in the graph to show the temperature for the past five days.

	Monday	Tuesday	Wednesday	Thursday	Friday
120					
110					
100					
90					
80					
70					
60					
50					
40					
30					
20					
10					
0					

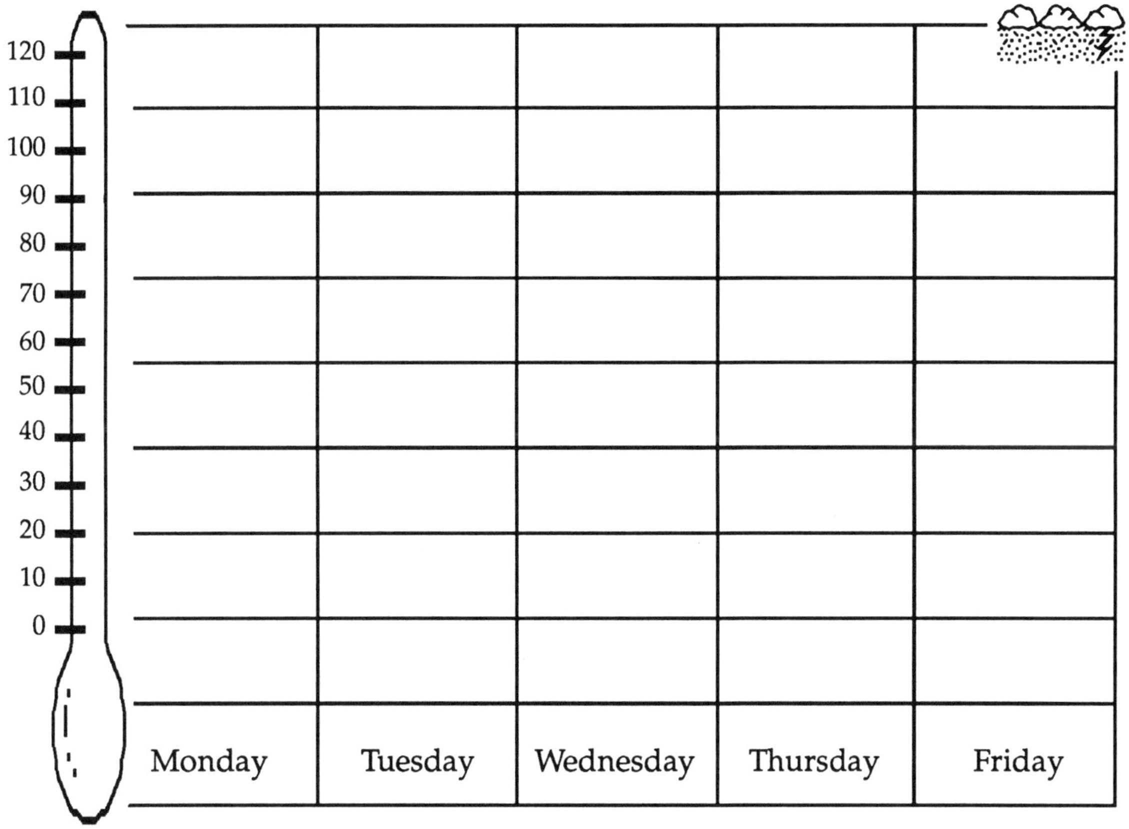

Which day of the week was coolest? _____

Which day of the week had the highest temperature? _____

What was the average temperature for the past five days? _____

How many days did it rain and/or snow? _____

What was the weather like when you got out of school on Wednesday?_____

Write one sentence to describe the weather for the past five days. _____

_____

_____

PERSONAL PROPERTY

An inventory is a listing of current assets. You may be surprised to realize what goods you have on hand at this very minute that make up your assets.

Check your desk, your pockets, purse, lunch box, locker, and any other place you may have property that belongs to you **at school** right now. List it all, and feel rich!

OF PERSONAL PROPERTY BELONGING TO:

_____ on _____
                    (Name)   (Date)

_____ _____ _____ _____

_____ _____ _____ _____

_____ _____ _____ _____

_____ _____ _____ _____

_____ _____ _____ _____

_____ _____ _____ _____

List the three most valuable items on your inventory sheet.

1. _____

2. _____

3. _____

Which is the most useful?

_____

YOU LIGHT UP THEIR LIVES

Name _____

    People who really care about other people learn to plan ahead to be able to bring happiness into the lives of others by remembering special occasions and events.

    On scrap paper, make a list of the people you will want to remember in a special way during the next year. Note the date, occasion, and an idea of what you might do to make it a special day for that person.

Example: **Jan. 7**   Aunt Iris   Birthday   Pretty card
              Feb. 6   Joey   Birthday   Model plane kit
              June 2 Marsha   Graduation   Lunch or flowers

    Arrange the list by date beginning with January, and copy it in the space below. Mount your SPECIAL OCCASIONS page on colored paper to take home as a reminder for the next year!

DATE	NAME	OCCASION	SPECIAL PLAN

Special Occasions Planner
© 1991 by Incentive Publications, Inc., Nashville, TN.

MINI-MESSAGES

Memo is short for memorandum. A memo is a very short message written to give some very specific information in the fewest words possible.

Write a memo on a separate sheet of paper for each of the messages below. Remember, use the fewest words possible, but make sure your memo tells what, when, where, and why.

The cookie chairman of Girl Scout Troop 92 needs to tell all scouts in the troop that cookies will go on sale Tuesday, May 14. The cookies should be picked up at her house, 114 Glendale Street, between 2 and 4 p.m. next Saturday.

The principal of your school wants to tell all teachers in the school that the halls are too noisy and that he wants fewer students in the main hall between classes.

The chief of the fire department needs to call a meeting of all volunteer firemen on Friday, July 13, at 3:30 p.m. at the main firehall.

Write a memo on a separate sheet of paper to tell your teacher something you think he/she should know (an important event, etc.).

Memoranda
© 1991 by Incentive Publications, Inc., Nashville, TN.

CHECKUP

Name _____

Heidi Harrison is a well-organized young lady who works hard and plans how to spend her money wisely. She has just opened her first checking account and is being very careful to live up to this new responsibility.

The banker reminded Heidi that a check is a written order telling the bank to take the sum of money specified from the account of the person who has signed the check. The banker also reminded Heidi to always remember to include:

1. Date.
2. Name of the person/company to receive the money.
3. Exact amount.
4. Signature.

Help Heidi by completing these checks. Use the months and days given, but add this year's date.

The National Nature Museum dues were due on July 19th. Heidi wrote a check that day for her $6 annual dues.

```
                                    _____ 19 _____
Pay to the
Order of _____ $ _____

_____ Dollars

For _____        _____
```

Heidi bought a notebook, three pencils, a pen, and a book bag from the Pierce School Bookstore. She wrote a check for $21.22 for her purchase on August 27th.

```
                                    _____ 19 _____
Pay to the
Order of _____ $ _____

_____ Dollars

For _____        _____
```

Writing Checks
© 1991 by Incentive Publications, Inc., Nashville, TN.

CHECKUP

Name _____

   Banking is serious business. Writing checks and keeping a checkbook balanced takes a little extra thought and effort at first, but it is a good way to keep a record of where and how you spend your money.

   Use this page from Heidi Harrison's checkbook. Enter the checks written by Heidi on the CHECKUP page and add the following deposits to practice some good banking business. Be sure to enter both the checks and deposits in order by date.

   On March 1st, Heidi deposited $19.29 that she earned from baby-sitting jobs.

Heidi sold her old roller skates and some books and records in a sidewalk sale for $16. She deposited this money on June 16th.

From her allowance, Heidi saved $7.50 which she deposited on July 1st.

Grandmother Harrison mailed Heidi a check for $22 for back-to-school expenses. Heidi deposited it on August 2nd.

How much money did Heidi have in her checking account on September 1st?

DATE	CHECK NUMBER	CHECKS ISSUED TO OR DEPOSIT RECEIVED FROM	AMOUNT OF DEPOSIT	✓	(-) CHECK FEE (IF ANY)	AMOUNT OF CHECK	BALANCE	

A SAFE DEPOSIT

Name _____

      Before you can withdraw money from a bank account by writing a check, you must put money in the bank. This is called making a deposit. For each deposit, a deposit slip must be completed so that the bank will know exactly how much money to add to which account.

      Fill in the deposit record for each of the following:

	DOLLARS	CENTS
CURRENCY		
COIN		
CHECKS		
TOTAL FROM OTHER SIDE		
TOTAL		
LESS CASH RECEIVED		
TOTAL		

three $20 bills
two $5 bills
check for $12
check for $43.28

	DOLLARS	CENTS
CURRENCY		
COIN		
CHECKS		
TOTAL FROM OTHER SIDE		
TOTAL		
LESS CASH RECEIVED		
TOTAL		

1 $10 bill
5 quarters
check for $76.89

one $50 bill
two $10 bills
checks for: $2.75, $4.50, $26.95

	DOLLARS	CENTS
CURRENCY		
COIN		
CHECKS		
TOTAL FROM OTHER SIDE		
TOTAL		
LESS CASH RECEIVED		
TOTAL		

$7 in bills
10 quarters
2 dimes
checks for $100, $16.50

	DOLLARS	CENTS
CURRENCY		
COIN		
CHECKS		
TOTAL FROM OTHER SIDE		
TOTAL		
LESS CASH RECEIVED		
TOTAL		

ANATOMY OF A BIOGRAPHY

PURPOSE:
Collecting and organizing factual data

PREPARATION:

1. Reproduce the BIOGRAPHICAL DATA and EDITOR'S GUIDE work sheets.

PROCEDURE:

1. Discuss the elements of a good biography, and if necessary, give examples by displaying biographies of famous people well-known to the students.

2. Pair students to write each other's biography.

3. Distribute copies of the BIOGRAPHICAL DATA and EDITOR'S GUIDE work sheets.

4. Direct students to:
1. Interview the person whose biography they will write.
2. Complete the data sheet.
3. Write the biography and include the author's name.
4. Do a self-evaluation of the biography using the EDITOR'S GUIDE.

5. Collect completed biographies, and hold them for use in the PUBLISHER'S LISTING activity.

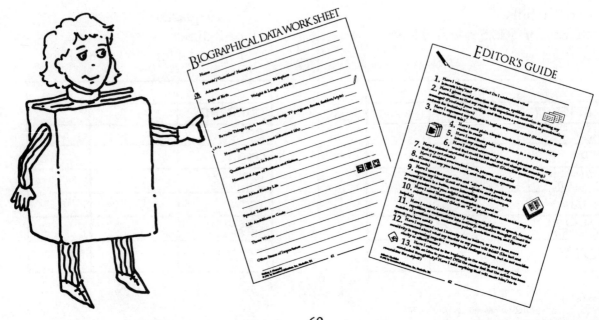

BIOGRAPHICAL DATA WORK SHEET

Name _____

Parents'/Guardians' Name(s) _____

Address _____

Date of Birth _____ Birthplace _____

Time_____ Weight & Length at Birth _____

Schools Attended _____

_____

Favorite Things (sport, book, movie, song, TV program, foods, fashion/style) _____

_____

Heroes (people who have most influenced life) _____

_____

Qualities Admired in Friends _____

Names and Ages of Brothers and Sisters _____

_____

Notes About Family Life _____

_____

Special Talents _____

Life Ambitions or Goals _____

_____

Three Wishes _____

_____

Other Items of Importance _____

_____

Writing A Biography
© 1991 by Incentive Publications, Inc., Nashville, TN.

EDITOR'S GUIDE

1. Have I visualized my reader? Do I understand what interests him/her?

2. Have I given careful attention to grammar, spelling, and punctuation so that my reader will experience no confusion in getting my message? (Proofread your writing, and then have a person skilled in proofreading recheck for technical errors.)

3. Have I expressed my thoughts in logical, sequential order? (Number the main ideas to check this.)

4. Have I used plain, simple words that are comfortable for my reader to read?

5. Have I used those plain, simple words in a way that will interest my reader?

6. Have I deleted unnecessary words and phrases? (Circle any word that could be left out and not change the meaning.)

7. Have I deleted unrelated or irrelevant matter? (Underline sentences or phrases that may not relate.)

8. Have I avoided overworked words, phrases, and clichés? (Cross out any you have used, and write a better synonym above each.)

9. Have I used the most active and "alive" words possible to express my ideas? (Look at each adjective and adverb. Ask yourself if there is a better, more interesting, more picturesque, or more precise word you might substitute.)

10. Have I used illustrations or examples to expand or reinforce main ideas? (Mark an "X" at places where such entries may be helpful.)

11. Have I created/added interest by interspersing figures of speech, forceful repetition, or exclamations into ordinary, declarative thought? (Count the number of question marks, exclamation points, quotation marks, and figures of speech you have used.)

12. Have I expressed what I honestly feel or believe, or have I been more concerned about what my teacher or my peers will think? (Use tact and sensitivity in expressing negative or unpopular feelings or ideas, but do not sacrifice clarity or effectiveness.)

13. Have I referred to the beginning in the ending and left my reader with an idea to ponder? (Will the reader feel that the article has been concluded thoughtfully? Have I said anything that will cause him/her to reconsider the subject?)

PUBLISHER'S LISTING

PURPOSE:
Writing a bibliography/proofreading

PREPARATION:

1. Assemble construction paper, felt-tip pens, and staplers for the students. Glue the STUDY GUIDE to a piece of tagboard.

2. Laminate or place in an acetate sleeve the pages, PROOFREADER'S MARKS and EDITOR'S GUIDE.

3. Place all materials in a learning center setting (or modify instructions and use as a directed-teaching or homework activity).

PROCEDURE:

1. Lead a class discussion related to publishing original writing. Display copies of two or three books of interest to the students, calling attention to the copyright page.

2. To acquaint students with bibliographic form, ask each to take a book from his/her desk, turn to the copyright page, and make a bibliographic listing for the book. (You may need to write one on the chalkboard for reference.)

Example: Forte, Imogene. *Skillstuff - Reading.* Nashville:
Incentive Publications, Inc., 1979.

3. Use your grade or room number as a publishing company name (example: Seventh Grade Publications), and direct students to complete the learning center tasks in their free time.

4. Elect a committee to make a bibliography of all the biographies completed in the ANATOMY OF A BIOGRAPHY activity. Also elect a proofreading committee.

5. Review procedures for proofreading with the entire group. (See the page entitled PROOFREADER'S MARKS, and use that as a guide for making a set for your bulletin board.)

6. Place the proofed and corrected bibliography and all completed biographies in the learning center. Provide time and encourage all students to use the correct bibliography to select at least three or four biographies to read.

PUBLISHER'S LISTING
STUDY GUIDE

1. Reread the biography you have just completed. Correct any errors in spelling or punctuation. Use the questions in the EDITOR'S GUIDE to evaluate and improve your work.

2. Give your biography a catchy name.

3. Select a color of paper, and use felt-tip pens to design a cover. Make your cover as attractive as possible to encourage people to read your book.

4. Make a title page and a copyright page for your book.

5. Staple your book together.

6. Complete a bibliography card for your book. Remember to give the following information and to use the correct punctuation.

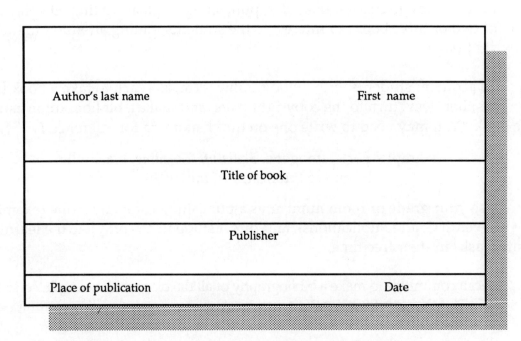

Author's last name	First name
Title of book	
Publisher	
Place of publication	Date

7. An annotated bibliography contains a very brief description of each book. Write a two or three sentence annotation for your book on the back of your bibliography card.

PROOFREADERS MARKS

Instruction	Mark in Margin	Mark in type	Corrected Type
Delete	℘	the ~~good~~ word	the word
Insert indicated material	good	the word	the good word
Let it stand	stet	the good word	the good word
Make capital	cap	the word	the Word
Make lower case	lc	The word	the Word
Set in small capitals	SC	See word.	See WORD.
Set in italic type	ital	The word is word.	The word is *word*.
Set in roman type	rom	the (word)	the word
Set in boldface type	bf	the entry word	the entry **word**
Set in lightface type	lf	the entry word	the entry word
Transpose	tr	the word good	the good word
Close up space	◠	the wo rd	the word
Delete and close up space	℘	the word	the word
Spell out	sp	②words	two words
Insert: space	#	theword	the word
period	⊙	This is the word	This is the word.
comma	⋀	words words, words	words, words, words
hyphen	⸗	word for word test	word-for-word test
colon	⊙	The following words	The following words:
semicolon	⌃	Scan the words skim the words.	Scan the words; skim the words.
apostrophe	⋁	Johns words	John's words
quotation marks	⌣/⌣/	the word word	the word "word"
parentheses	(/) /	The word word is in parentheses.	The word (word) is in parentheses.
brackets	[/] /	He read from the Word the Bible.	He read from the Word [the Bible].
en dash	⊣N⊢	1964 1972	1964-1972
em dash	⊣M⊢/⊣M⊢/	The dictionary how often it is needed belongs in every home.	The dictionary—how often it is needed— belongs in every home.
superior type	⌄	$2' = 4$	$2^2 = 4$
inferior type	⌃	$H_{}0$	H_2O
asterisk	⋁	word	word*
dagger	†	a word	a word†
double dagger	‡	words and words	words and words‡
section symbol	§	Book Reviews	§ Book Reviews
virgule	/	either or	either/or
Start paragraph	¶	"Where is it?" "It's on the shelf."	"Where is it?" "It's on the shelf."
Run in	run in	The entry word is printed in boldface. The pronunciation follows.	The entry word is printed in boldface. The pronunciation follows.
Turn right side up	⊙	the word	the word
Move left	[	the word	the word
Move right	]	the word	the word
Move up	⊓	the word	the word
Move down	⊔	the word	the word
Align	‖	the word the word the word	the word the word the word
Straighten line	=	the word	the word
Wrong font	wf	the word	the word
Broken type	x	the word	the word

© 1978 by Houghton Mifflin Company. Reprinted by permission from *The American Heritage Dictionary of the English Language*.

A LETTER FOR A FRIEND

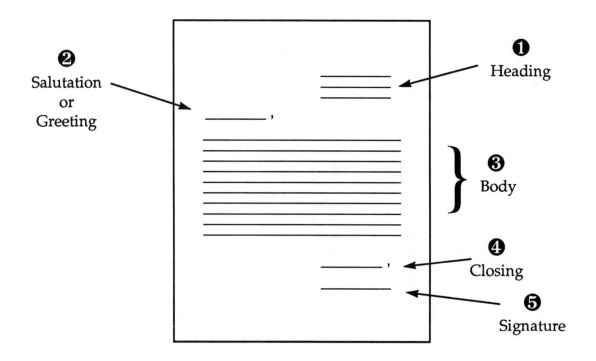

The diagram above will help you review the five important parts of a friendly letter. This is the form used to write friends, family, and other nonbusiness acquaintances.

Now pretend you and five friends are on a camping trip in a national park. You want to share your adventures with a special buddy at home. Using the friendly letter form, write a note that tells your friend about some of your experiences.

Here's what's happened:

- You caught three fish and cooked them for breakfast.
- You saw huge sequoia trees. It took all six of you holding hands to circle one of the trunks with your arms!
- While you were napping a bear "borrowed" your backpack and ate your lunch, your toothpaste, and half your hat!
- You made a log bridge to cross a stream.
- You played with bullfrogs in a mountain lake.
- You saw several deer, loons, and a trumpeter swan.

Note: Choose from this list and add some adventures of your own to create a letter that is fun and interesting for your friend to read.

Form Of A Friendly Letter
© 1991 by Incentive Publications, Inc., Nashville, TN.

THE SOCIAL SET

Name _____

    A social note may be formal (very polite and proper) or informal (more relaxed and friendly). It may be as long or short as the sender wants it. The important thing about a social note is that it must carry the intended message.

    Write a social note for each of the situations below.

It's a Party!

Thank You

An invitation to your birthday party

A thank-you note

Seems Like A Long Time...

A "just to keep in touch" note to someone in another town

MESSAGES IN BRIEF

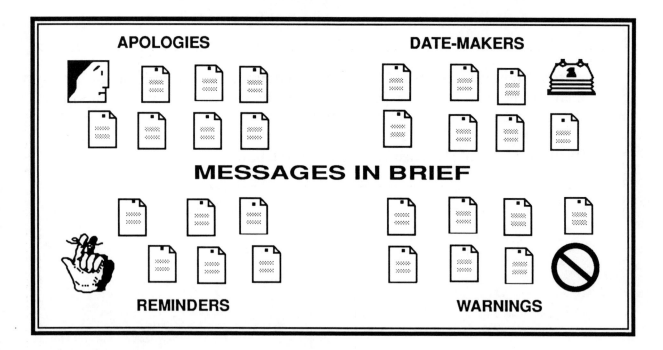

PURPOSE:
Writing brief, informal messages

PREPARATION:

1. Using the above model, create a writing center or bulletin board exhibiting the four symbols that represent reminders, apologies, dates, and warnings.

2. Make a copy of the MESSAGES IN BRIEF work sheet for each student.

PROCEDURE:

1. Distribute a copy of the MESSAGES IN BRIEF work sheet to each student.

2. Discuss with students the nature and purpose of brief, informal notes emphasizing clear, concise communication.

3. Ask each student to use the work sheet to create at least three of the four suggested notes, then cut out and attach each of their notes to the corresponding parts of the teacher-prepared bulletin board.

4. Ask students to read the notes at their leisure and decide whether the message of each note is presented clearly and concisely. Students should enjoy reading one another's creative contributions!

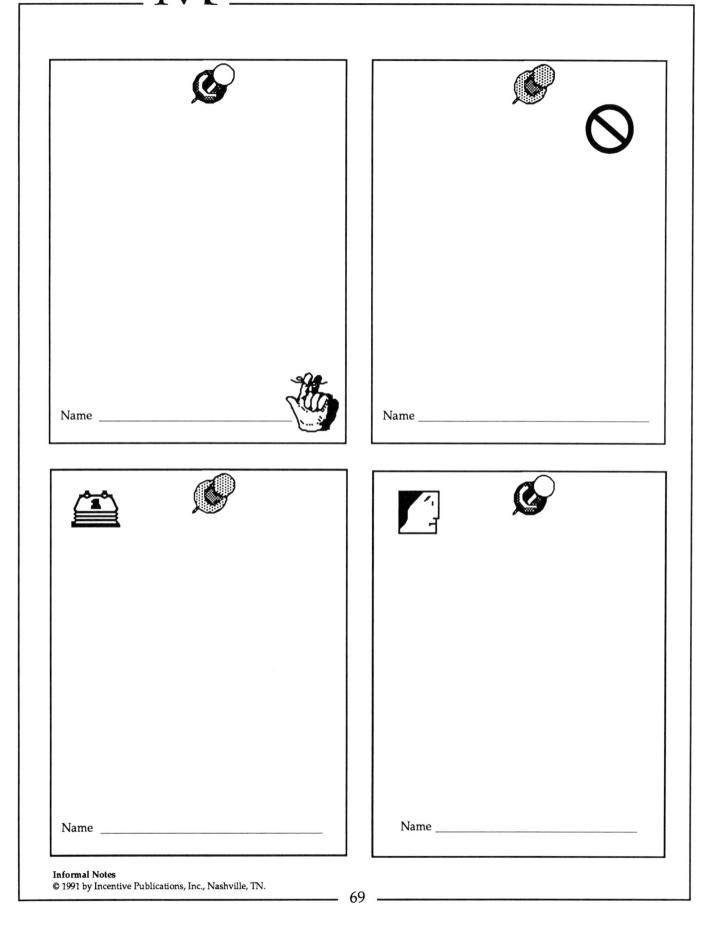

Name _____

Name _____

Name _____

Name _____

Informal Notes
© 1991 by Incentive Publications, Inc., Nashville, TN.

A GLIMPSE OF PARADISE

A picture postcard is a special medium for sending messages. It allows the writer to communicate in two ways – choosing a picture message for his reader to enjoy and creating a word message for him to read. But its size and form make special demands on the writer.

1. Because of limited space, the message must be brief and concise.

2. Confine the message to only the left side of the writing surface of the card. The right side is reserved for the address and postage. (Post offices in some countries refuse to accept cards on which the message spills over onto the address side of the card.)

Pretend you are a traveler to a faraway, exotic place. Use the space on this side of the postcard to write your message. Properly address the card. On the blank side, glue a picture cut from a travel magazine or draw a picture that will show something about the place you have chosen to "visit." Make it a fun card for your intended receivers!

From:

To:

Postcards
© 1991 by Incentive Publications, Inc., Nashville, TN.

A MATTER OF BUSINESS

A business letter is very much like a friendly letter. The difference is that it has one additional part – the language is more formal and polite and the punctuation is slightly different. The business letter has six parts.

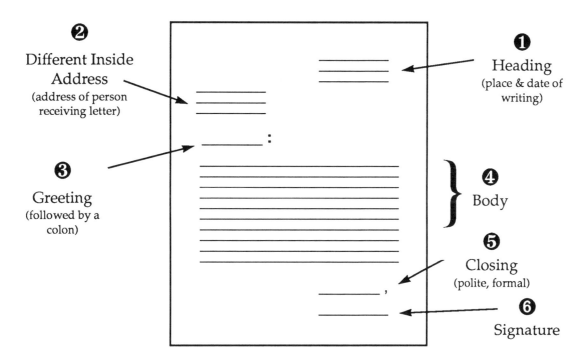

❷ Different Inside Address
(address of person receiving letter)

❸ Greeting
(followed by a colon)

❶ Heading
(place & date of writing)

❹ Body

❺ Closing
(polite, formal)

❻ Signature

1. Use your own paper to write a business letter.

2. Choose the situation that interests you most on the A MATTER OF BUSINESS situations page.

3. Write your letter in business form. Be brief and courteous. Tell exactly what you want, and be sure to give all the information needed.

4. Fold your letter in three parts as shown below (folding the bottom up first), and properly address the outside as you would an envelope.

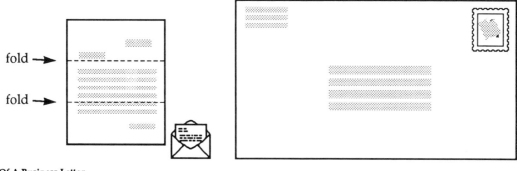

fold →

fold →

I. Last summer at a party, you saw a singing birthday card that was a big hit with teenagers. One of your best friends is having a birthday and you can't locate a singing card anywhere. The local card shop suggests that you might find out where such cards can be purchased by writing to Magic Moments, Inc., 785 Star Lane, Rainbow, Rhode Island 21703.

II. You are very concerned about the conservation of natural resources. Recently you have noticed that a chain store being built in four locations in your city is ripping out hundreds of trees and replacing them with huge concrete parking lots. You believe some of the trees could be saved and that new plants could be attractively arranged in "islands" throughout the parking lots. You want to share your concerns and ideas with the head of the company Mrs. Roger Rant at 300 Mega Plaza in Atlanta, Georgia 30062.

III. A science magazine headquarters located in Tampa, Florida, advertises an ant farm complete with ants. It is only $9.95. You've always wanted an ant farm for your bedroom, but you need to know how large it is and whether it is possible to order additional ants at a later time. The company, Science & More, is located at 1800 North Third Street. The zip code is 47029.

IV. You are a big fan of heavy metal music. A friend has told you about a discount record shop that specializes in heavy metal. You would like to receive a catalog of all the records they sell. Your friend gives you this address: Metal Media, Inc., 143 Disc Drive, Los Angeles, California 94073.

V. You have started an organization called GRIT (Get Rid of Idle Talk). You hate the silly inside joking and smutty innuendos made by early-morning talk show hosts and disc jockeys in your area. They make morning radio sound like locker room talk. You think they should clean up their act, and you plan to write your local radio station and tell them so in a strong but businesslike manner.

VI. A cereal box offers a collection of mechanical outer-space creatures. They would make a great birthday gift for your little brother, but the box offers only one at a time. You wonder if it's possible to purchase the entire set, how much it would cost, and how fast the order could be shipped by The Far Out Company, 1001 Inter-Galactic Circle, Mars, Pennsylvania 30400.

Sherri Campbell
Rt. 3 Box 111-G
Small Town, USA

The Far Out Company
1001 Inter-Galactic Circle
Mars, Pennsylvania 30400

Kevin Crownover
123 Rambling Lane
Smaller Town, USA

The Metal Media, Inc.
143 Disc Drive
Los Angeles, CA 94073

Sara Lewis
Rt. 2 Box 114-B
Small Town, USA

Science & More
1800 North Third Street
Tampa, Florida 47029

Scott Smith
166 Elm Street
Tiny Town, USA

Magic Moments Company
785 Star Lane
Rainbow, RI 21703

INFORMATION PLEASE

Name _____

     Julie Jacobsky lives at 913 West Iris Lane in Chicago, Illinois 60602. She wrote a business letter to the Heartland Art Company, 919 Marymount Avenue in St. Paul, Minnesota 55116 to request a catalog and to ask how long it should take for a shipment from the company to reach her.

     Write Julie's letter in the space below. Use today's date.

WHOOPS!

Name _____

Julie addressed an envelope for her letter like this:

Her mother looked at the envelope and said that it would never be delivered. She reminded Julie that the Heartland Art Company in St. Paul, Minnesota, is located at 919 Marymount Avenue, and the zip code is 55116.

Readdress her envelope correctly. (Don't forget capital letters and punctuation.)

I'M SOMETHING SPECIAL

Name _____

    You are the only person in the world exactly like you, and that makes you unique. That's also what makes you interesting to other people. Think about the things that make you just a little different than everyone else. That's the stuff a good autobiography is made of!

Think about:

BASIC STUFF:

When and where you were born
Where you've lived
Schools you've attended

BETTER STUFF:

Special people in your life
Family and friends
Heroes – such as a teacher, coach, movie star, etc.

PERSONAL STUFF:

Strong and weak characteristics
Special talents and abilities
Special interests, likes and dislikes

MEMORABLE STUFF:

Your first trip   Pets
Best birthday or holiday   Deaths
Moving to a new house   Surprises
Starting in a new school   Changes
Embarrassing moments   Winning something
Treasured possessions   Losing something

FUTURE STUFF:

Hopes, dreams
Career
Ambitions

    Reread this list and make notes beside the items that spark ideas for your own life story. Then use scrap paper to organize your ideas and create a rough draft. When you have refined and edited your story, use the title "I'm Something Special" and recopy your story on a clean sheet of paper. Writing an autobiography is a great opportunity. It allows you to describe exactly the person you want the world to know as YOU!

DAY BY DAY

PURPOSE:
Conceiving and verbalizing by keeping a daily journal.

PREPARATION:

1. Ask each student to bring a notebook to be used only for keeping a daily journal.

2. Read several short excerpts from journals (such as *The Diary of Anne Frank*) to the class. Discuss the special kind of thinking and writing that are peculiar to journal writing, i.e., personal and private, but in this case, something that may be read by the teacher. Mention several kinds of things students might want to record such as daily happenings they'd like to remember, feelings, goals to work toward, new ideas, poems, etc.

Emphasize the difference between a journal and a diary. (A journal is a broader collection of ideas to treasure. These ideas do not have to be original with the journal writer. A diary is more of an account of the actual experiences and thoughts of the writer.) As an example, ask class members to contribute real or pretend journal entries. Write them on the chalkboard. The teacher should contribute, too!

PROCEDURE:

1. Set aside a 5-10 minute period each day for students to write three or four sentence entries in their journals. Emphasize that the journals will not be corrected; however, the teacher may write a brief comment after a week's entries.

2. Ask students to date each entry. Encourage them to be neat and to add any special drawings, cartoons, or hieroglyphics they wish. [They may also wish to address each entry, i.e., "Dear Self," or "Dear (name)."]

3. Collect journals once a week (or a few each day) to observe each student's progress in language skills and personal understanding. Special needs for skill development will become apparent in the process. (These journals also make an excellent basis for parent/teacher conferences.)

Note: By all means, keep a daily journal yourself, and make it available for the students to read while you are reading theirs. Use it to set an example of interesting, humor-laced, meaningful writing. It's also a good way to let students know some of your feelings and to emphasize good values.

DEAR DIARY

PURPOSE:
Writing a diary

PREPARATION:

1. Reproduce copies of the MAKE IT SPARKLE and the TODAY IS THE DAY work sheets.

PROCEDURE:

1. Lead a class discussion of the value of keeping a diary, emphasizing such aspects as:

1. Personal pleasure
2. Self-discipline
3. Improvement in writing skills and style
4. Having a permanent record of daily events
5. Being able to read back over you own life story at a future time

2. Read and discuss excerpts from the diaries of some famous people.
Diary of an Edwardian Lady   *Diary of Anne Frank*
Diary of Evelyn Waugh   *Diary of Tchaikovsky*

3. Distribute copies of the MAKE IT SPARKLE work sheet.

4. Allow time for students to read the work sheet and answer questions.

5. Discuss ways people observe what is happening around them and develop sensitivity to people and events in their environments and how this makes a difference in their attitudes and beliefs.

6. Distribute copies of TODAY IS THE DAY to be used as a homework assignment (and don't forget to plan time for follow-up).

MAKE IT SPARKLE!

Name _____

     Justin and Josephine are good friends. They live on the same street and are in the same grade. As they walked to school one day, they decided to share their diaries.

     Here are some sample pages from each diary.

Monday, Oct. 10

    We rode the bus to the zoo. It was a great field trip —I was fascinated by the baby elephant—Justin said that the snakes were hibernating and that is why they were so still—I'm not sure that is true.

    Jennie and I ate lunch together and found we really have a lot in common. I made an "A" on my spelling test. Dad says he's really proud of my improvement.

Tuesday, Oct. 11

    Boy, was this day a downer! First, I forgot my lunch money. Next I did the wrong math pages for homework. Well, at least my teacher understood. After school I played kickball with Justin and Jackson—later the three of us went to the soda shop for ice cream cones. We seem to be getting along better now; I think it's because we're growing up.

    Grandma came for supper and told us all about her new neighbors the Seligman's who moved from California.

Monday, Oct. 10

    Went on a class field trip to the zoo. The animals were interesting.

    Got my paper back from last week's spelling test.

    We had guests for dinner and had a lot of special stuff to eat.

Tuesday, Oct. 11

    Just a usual day —school was sort of boring. After school we played kickball in the backyard and had fun.

    After dinner I did homework, watched a little TV, took my bath, and went to bed at my usual time.

Whose diary is more interesting to read and why? _____

_____

List three experiences that you know Justin had because Josephine recorded them in her diary.

1. _____

2. _____

3. _____

What advice would you give Justin? _____

_____

_____

TODAY IS THE DAY

Name _____

    Write a page for your diary for today. Think over all the interesting things that happened, and decide what you want to remember.

    Since a diary is a very personal bit of writing, you will want to use your space for only those things that you think are worth recording. Thoughts, questions, quotations, and feelings are important, too. Add a picture or two if you like. Remember, it's **your** life you are writing about, and you are not a dull person!

Writing Skills Checklist

NAME _____ GRADE _____ DATE _____

TEACHER _____

WRITING PARAGRAPHS
- ❑ Writing Topic Sentences
- ❑ Organizing a Paragraph

PARTS OF SPEECH
- ❑ Nouns
- ❑ Verbs
- ❑ Adjectives
- ❑ Adverbs
- ❑ Words Used as More Than One Part of Speech

WORD USAGE
- ❑ Synonyms, Antonyms,
- ❑ Homonyms
- ❑ Multiple Meanings
- ❑ Comparisons
- ❑ Plurals and Possessives
- ❑ Preciseness
- ❑ Abbreviations and Contractions
- ❑ Avoid Cliches
- ❑ Internalizing Word Meanings
- ❑ Overworked Words

USING PUNCTUATION MARKS
- ❑ End Punctuation
- ❑ Commas

- ❑ Apostrophes
- ❑ Quotation Marks
- ❑ Colons and Semicolons
- ❑ Parentheses

USING CAPITAL LETTERS
- ❑

SPELLING
- ❑

WRITING SENTENCES
- ❑ Four Kinds of Sentences
- ❑ Writing a Good Sentence
- ❑ Fragments, Complete Sentences
- ❑ Run-on Sentences
- ❑ Subject/Verb Agreement
- ❑ Parallel Construction
- ❑ Writing topic Sentences
- ❑ Organizing a Paragraph

ORGANIZING IDEAS
- ❑ Using a Variety of Resources
- ❑ Sequencing Thoughts
- ❑ Note-Taking, Summarizing
- ❑ Paraphrasing
- ❑ Precis Writing